The Fun Trip Guide to

MACHU PICCHU

101+ Fun Activities and Must-see Attractions Suitable for Visitors of all Ages

With travel checklist and budget planner

Amy T. Moore

Copyright

All rights reserved. No part of this publication may be reproduced, distributed, or transmitted in any form or by any means, including photocopying, recording, or other electronic or mechanical methods, without the prior written permission of the publisher, except in the case of brief quotations embodied in critical reviews and certain other noncommercial uses permitted by copyright law.

Copyright © Amy T. Moore, 2023.

Table of Content

Introduction.. 8
    Brief History.. 12
    Machu Picchu Fun Facts..................................... 16
    Packing Essentials.. 18
Part A: Must See Attractions............................ 22
    1. Machu Picchu Citadel..................................... 22
    2. Huayna Picchu.. 24
    3. Sun Gate (Inti Punku)..................................... 25
    4. Temple of the Sun.. 25
    5. Temple of The Three Windows..................... 26
    6. The Main Plaza... 27
    7. The Inca Bridge.. 28
    8. The Inca Trail... 29
    9. Agricultural Terraces...................................... 31
    10. The Watchman's Hut................................... 32
    11. Temple of the Condor:................................. 33
    12. Intihuatana Stone:....................................... 34
    13. Royal Tomb:... 35
    14. Funerary Rock Hut:..................................... 36
    15. Guardhouse Ruins:...................................... 37
    16. Huayna Picchu Temple................................ 38
    17. Temple of the Moon.................................... 39
    18. Room of the Three Doors:........................... 39
    19. Sayacmarca Ruins....................................... 40
    20. Putucusi Mountain...................................... 41
    21. Inca Drawbridge.. 42

22. Wiñay Wayna Ruins..43
23. Machu Picchu Museum..44
24. Machu Picchu Gateway Museum:......................45
Part B: Fun Things To Do...................................47
25. Hike the Inca Trail..47
26. Explore the Sacred Valley............................... 48
27. Hike to the Sun Gate:....................................... 48
28. Climb Huayna Picchu.. 49
29. Visit the Putucusi Mountain............................ 50
30. Trek to the Temple of the Moon:................... 50
31. Bird watching in the Cloud Forest:................. 51
32. River Rafting in Urubamba River:................... 52
33. Zipline through the Cloud Forest:....................53
34. Horseback Riding Tours:................................. 54
35. Mountain Biking:...54
36. Enjoy a Scenic Picnic:......................................55
37. Hot Springs in Aguas Calientes:......................56
38. Attend a Traditional Andean ceremony:........... 56
39. Visit Local Markets in Aguas Calientes:............57
40. Learn about Andean Textiles:..........................58
41. Taste Some Andean Food:...............................58
42. Participate in a Pachamama Ceremony:........... 61
43. Watch Traditional Dance Performances:.......... 62
44. Visit the Museo de Sitio Manuel Chávez Ballón:... 62
45. Explore the Orchid Botanical Garden:...............63
46. Go check out the Butterfly House!..................64
47. Sunrise and Sunset Photography:.....................65
48. Scenic Views of the Urubamba River:............... 65

4

49. Wildlife Photography...66
50. Capture the llamas and Alpacas.........................67
51. Stunning Agricultural Terraces......................... 67
52. Ancient Stone Structures:.................................. 68
53. Misty Mountain Landscapes:.............................69
54. Cloud Forest Flora:..70
55. Train Ride through the Valley:...........................70
56. Paragliding over Machu Picchu:........................ 71
57. Rock Climbing in the Region:............................72
58. Explore the Caves Near Machu Picchu:..............72
59. Mountain Biking on Inca Trails:........................ 73
60. Canopy and Zip-lining Adventures:...................74
61. White-water rafting in Urubamba River:...........74
62. Via Ferrata Climbing and Zipline:..................... 75
63. Birdwatching in the Cloud Forest:..................... 75
64. Spot Orchids and Native Flora:..........................76
65. Llama and Alpaca Encounters:.......................... 77
66. Monkey Watching in the Forest:........................77
67. Butterfly Spotting:..78
68. Andean Condor Watching:.................................79
69. Soak in the Aguas Calientes Hot Springs:.......... 80
70. Yoga and Meditation Retreats:.......................... 80
71. Spa and Wellness Centers:..................................81
72. Forest Bathing in the Cloud Forest:................... 81
73. Aguas Calientes Town Exploration:....................82
74. Explore Ollantaytambo:...................................... 83
75. Visit Pisac and its Market:..................................83
76. Discover Chinchero Village:...............................84
77. Explore Urubamba Village:................................ 84

5

78. Santa Teresa Village:.. 85
79. Hike to Santa Teresa Hot Springs:..................... 86
80 . Explore the Maras Salt Ponds:......................... 86
81. Visit Moray Agricultural Terraces:..................... 87
82. Explore the Ruins of Ollantaytambo................ 87
83. Nighttime Stargazing Tours............................. 88
84. Learn About Inca Astronomy........................... 89
85. Take a Guided Tour of Machu Picchu.............. 89
86. Hire a Local Guide for In-depth Insights:......... 90
87. Attend Workshops and Lectures:...................... 91
88. Visit the Local Schools and Communities:........ 92
89. Attend Workshops on Traditional Andean Pottery:... 92
90. Learn about Andean Agriculture:..................... 93
91. Traditional Andean Cooking Classes:............... 94
92. Spanish Language Classes:.............................. 94
93. Check for Local Festivals and Events:.............. 95
94. Inti Raymi (Festival of the Sun):....................... 95
95. Cusco's Annual Celebrations:........................... 96
96. Buy Traditional Andean Textiles:..................... 97
97. Purchase Handmade Crafts:............................ 97
98. Unique Machu Picchu Souvenirs:..................... 98
99. Plan Your Next Adventure in the Andes:........... 99
100. Explore Other Inca ruins in Peru:................... 99
101. Visit Cusco, the Historic Capital of the Inca Empire:.. 100
Key Details:... 100
102. Explore the Amazon Rainforest:.................... 101
103. Trek to Salkantay or Ausangate:................... 102

6

104. Visit Lake Titicaca:... 102
105. Go sandboarding in Huacachina:....................103
Conclusion:..104
Travel Checklist
Budget Planner

Introduction

Dear Traveler,

Allow me to take you to Machu Picchu, a breathtaking location that will always have a special place in my heart. I'm excited to introduce you to this amazing place, where history, nature, and mysticism all come together, as a fellow traveler.

I started my adventure to Machu Picchu in Cusco, the former Inca Empire capital. When I stepped onto the train headed for Aguas Calientes, the entry point to Machu Picchu, I recall feeling excited. The train journey itself was a breathtaking sight, winding through the Andes and providing views of verdant landscapes and thunderous rivers.

I was ecstatic when I finally arrived at Aguas Calientes, a little village tucked away at the base of Machu Picchu in a cloud forest. There was a tangible sense of anticipation as other passengers got ready for the climb. I set out for the famous ruins early the next morning in the shadow of night. The Urubamba River's soothing murmur guided me throughout the journey, which was nothing short of wonderful.

With the first rays of morning breaking through the clouds, the ancient stone monuments of Machu Picchu gradually revealed themselves. I was astounded to see this Inca stronghold sitting atop a mountain. The encounter was enhanced by the enigmatic atmosphere created by the mist that often shrouds the location.

I spent hours discovering all the hidden gems of Machu Picchu, including terraced fields that rolled down the side of the mountain, elaborate masonry, and hallowed temples. Among my favorite places were the Temple of the Sun, with its carefully carved stones, and the mysterious Intihuatana stone, which is said to be an astronomical observatory.

Naturally, I gave in to the allure of ascending Huayna Picchu, the imposing mountain offering a bird's-eye perspective of Machu Picchu. The views of the fortress and the surrounding mountains made the long and difficult hike well worth it.

In addition to its historical importance, Machu Picchu is a wildlife preserve. Numerous flower, butterfly, and bird species may be found in the nearby cloud forest. I was astounded by the peaceful coexistence of nature and this historic city as I strolled through the verdant foliage.

I retired to the quaint village of Aguas Calientes in the evenings, where I had a well-earned dip in the hot springs and feasted on delectable Peruvian food. This little town's feeling of togetherness, along with its kind residents and other tourists, gave my trip a cozy and welcome feel.

Machu Picchu is a place that offers more than just tourists. You can connect with the spirit of the Andes and sense the echoes of a bygone period there. I was filled with a deep feeling of amazement and thankfulness for the chance to see such a miracle after the encounter.

I can only hope that, like mine, dear traveler, your trip to Machu Picchu is as breathtaking as mine will be. Don't forget to take your time, experience the enchantment of this location, and allow it to deeply impact your spirit.

Happy travels!

Amy T. Moore.

Brief History

The history of Machu Picchu is a tapestry laced with mystery, intrigue, and astounding accomplishment. Allow me to take you on a tour of this famous Inca citadel's extensive and intriguing past as you get ready to visit it.

Cultural Revolution:
The Inca Empire, which ruled over the Andes of South America beginning in the early 15th century, reached its zenith when Machu Picchu was constructed. Machu Picchu is evidence of the Incas' inventiveness and their reputation for sophisticated engineering and architecture.

Building and Objective:
In the fifteenth century, during the rule of Inca monarch Pachacuti, Machu Picchu was built. The settlement was painstakingly constructed on an Andean elevation with a view of the Urubamba River Valley. Its exact structure, made of large stones that fit together without the need for cement, still confounds engineers and archaeologists.

There is ongoing discussion on Machu Picchu's purpose. Despite being called the "Lost City of the Incas," it was probably a royal estate, a refuge for the Inca nobility, and a hub for agriculture and ceremonies. Some people think it was an observatory for astronomy and a site of religious importance.

Planning and Design:
The architectural aspects of Machu Picchu are magnificent. The city is separated into two primary sectors: the urban sector, which is home to temples, plazas, and residential structures, and the agricultural sector, which has terraced fields. Among the buildings of note are the Room of the Three Windows, the Temple of the Sun, and the Intihuatana stone, which is thought to be a ceremonial stone connected to astronomy.

Feats of Inca Engineering:
The Incas were experts in modifying their buildings to fit their surroundings. The agricultural terraces of Machu Picchu show how well the locals have adapted to the precipitous mountain slopes. These terraces avoided landslides and erosion in addition to providing nourishment.

Retreat and Abandonment:
Inexplicably, Machu Picchu was abandoned in the late 16th century, maybe as a result of a sickness epidemic or the Spanish invasion. It was shielded from the outer world by the dense cloud forest flora.

Hiram Bingham, an American historian and explorer, "rediscovered" Machu Picchu in 1911 with the assistance of native farmers in the area. His mission made this hidden gem known to the world, and as a result, it became acknowledged as one of the world's most significant archeological sites.

Site of UNESCO World Heritage:
Machu Picchu's historical and cultural value led to its designation as a UNESCO World Heritage Site in 1983. It attracts tourists from all over the world and is regarded as one of the New Seven Wonders of the World.

Maintenance and Conservation:
Machu Picchu has to deal with a number of issues, such as the effects of tourism and environmental damage. A lot of work has gone into ensuring both sustainable tourism and its protection. Strict guidelines and limits on visitor numbers are in place to preserve the integrity of the monument.

Machu Picchu Fun Facts

1. Lost City of the Incas: Built in the fifteenth century by the Inca ruler Pachacuti, Machu Picchu is often referred to as the "Lost City of the Incas".

2. Altitude Marvel: Nestled in the Peruvian Andes Mountains, Machu Picchu is one of the world's highest ancient monuments, rising to a height of around 2,430 meters (7,970 feet) above sea level.

3. Mysterious Abandonment: Historians continue to argue about the precise cause of the Incas' departure from Machu Picchu. There are hypotheses that attribute its abandonment to the

Spanish Conquest, while some believe an epidemic was the cause.

4. Architectural Marvel: Machu Picchu, with its carefully cut stones that fit together without the need for cement, is a demonstration of sophisticated Incan engineering. Many of the stones are still securely interlaced after centuries, demonstrating how impressively precise the building was.

5. Sacred Intihuatana Stone: Machu Picchu is home to a sacred Intihuatana stone, which is often referred to as a "hitching post of the sun." Astronomically speaking, it is said to be significant as a ceremonial stone connected to the sun.

6. Agricultural Terraces: The location has elaborate agricultural terraces that are intended to stop soil erosion in the high mountainous environment in addition to being used for farming.

7. Discovery by Hiram Bingham: Though local Quechua farmers were probably aware of its existence, Machu Picchu garnered worldwide notice when American historian and explorer Hiram Bingham rediscovered it in 1911.

8. UNESCO World Heritage Site: The cultural and historical value of Machu Picchu led to its designation as a UNESCO World Heritage Site in 1983.

9. Inca Trail Connection: The well-known Inca Trail is a strenuous but worthwhile trekking path that leads to Machu Picchu. It culminates in the magnificent sight of the ancient city and offers amazing vistas of the Andes.

10. Tourist Magnet: Millions of tourists visit Machu Picchu every year to take in its amazing beauty and wonder at its mysterious past. Today, it is a popular tourist attraction.

Packing Essentials

1. Comfortable Hiking Boots: - Robust footwear is essential, particularly if you want to explore the nearby trails.

2. Weather-appropriate Clothing: - Add layers to accommodate fluctuating temperatures.
   - A raincoat or poncho, as the weather is not always predictable.

3. Sun Protection: - Use a high SPF sunscreen.
   - A hat to shield the sun.

4. Comfy Walking Shoes: - Ideal for touring Machu Picchu on foot.

Equipment and Accessories: 1. Backpack: - Ideal for day excursions when carrying necessities.

2. Water Bottle: – Drink plenty of water while you explore.

3. Smartphone/Camera: - Take in the amazing vistas.

4. Snacks: - Energy bars, almonds, or other snacks for the ride.

Travel Documents: 1. Passport: - Verify the date of expiry.

2. Tickets and permissions: - Verify that you possess the required admission passes and permissions for Machu Picchu.

3. Identification and Copies: - Make photocopies and have identification on hand.

Health and Personal Care:1. Basic materials for small injuries are included in the First Aid Kit:.

2. Prescription drugs: - Always have prescriptions for any required drugs on hand.

3. Remedies for Altitude Sickness - Speak with a medical expert and think about preventing altitude sickness.

4. Toiletries: - Toiletries in travel-sized containers.

Miscellaneous:1. Make sure you can charge your gadgets with the Travel Adapter:.

2. Headlamp/Flashlight: - Handy if you want to explore early in the morning.

3. Travel Guides/Maps: - Bring along a reference book or map.

4. Money: - Local money in cash for modest purchases.

Optional: 1. Binoculars: - If you wish to examine the landscapes and birds up close.

2. Journal/Notebook: - Write down your ideas and recollections.

Don't forget to modify this list according to the time of year, the particular activities you have planned, and your own tastes. Make sure you always check the weather prediction for Machu Picchu at the time of your visit.

Part A: Must See Attractions

1. Machu Picchu Citadel

Key Information: - Often referred to as the "Lost City of the Incas," the crown gem of this archeological marvel is Machu Picchu Citadel. It is located at an altitude of around 2,430 meters (7,970 feet) above sea level. You must buy tickets well in advance in order to enter Machu Picchu.

The ordinary admission ticket and the Machu Picchu + Huayna Picchu/Machu Picchu + Mountain ticket are the two available ticket types.

The kind and season (high or low) have an impact on the price. The basic admission ticket costs around $50–60 while the Machu Picchu plus Huayna Picchu ticket is roughly $75–85.

Tips for Exploration:
-Get there early to avoid the crowds and see the captivating morning light. Around 5:30 AM, the first buses from Aguas Calientes depart.

Guided tours: For a more in-depth understanding of the history and importance of the location, think about hiring a local guide. There are guides provided at the front door.

Bring necessities: To capture the amazing vistas, remember to include a camera, water, sunscreen, a hat, and comfy shoes.

Follow defined trails: Please follow the official paths and refrain from climbing on the ruins in order to preserve the integrity of the site.

Time management: Machu Picchu can be explored in four hours on average. To maximize your visit, properly schedule your time.

2. Huayna Picchu

Key Information: The famous mountain that dominates Machu Picchu is called Huayna Picchu. There is a daily limit on the number of tourists to the strenuous walk.

You'll need to get a special permit in addition to your Machu Picchu admission ticket in order to summit Huayna Picchu. Since permits are highly sought after, reservations must be made well in advance. The price is around $15–20.

Adventure Advice:
Physical preparedness: The walk is strenuous due to its steep stairs and confined spaces. Make sure you are well equipped for this journey.

Two time slots: The entrance to Huayna Picchu is available from 7-8 AM and 10-11 AM. It's usually colder and gives better vistas in the early morning hours.

Magnificent views: The sweeping views of Machu Picchu from the peak are simply mesmerizing and provide a distinct viewpoint.

3. Sun Gate (Inti Punku)

Key Details: The Sun Gate, also called Inti Punku in Quechua, is an old Inca entryway that serves as the first point of entry for visitors coming to Machu Picchu along the Inca Trail. Your trekking plan will include a visit to the Sun Gate if you are walking the Inca Trail. Once within the citadel, individuals who don't want to climb may hike to the Sun Gate from Machu Picchu.

Tips for Exploration:
Distinct viewpoint: The Sun Gate provides an alternative viewpoint for seeing Machu Picchu. The climb is worthwhile and provides breathtaking views.
- The best time to visit the Sun Gate is in the late afternoon or early morning, when Machu Picchu is illuminated by warm, entrancing sunshine.

4. Temple of the Sun

Key Details:
The Temple of the Sun, often referred to as "Torreón" or "The Royal Mausoleum," is one of the most mysterious buildings in Machu Picchu.
- The structure is semicircular and has precisely cut stones that coincide with the solstices. For the

Incas, the temple had great religious and astrological significance.

Research Guidance:
Unique Design: Take in the Inca architectural expertise and the amazing curving masonry of the temple.

Solstice Alignment: Pay attention to the temple's particular orientation, since it is said to have been in line with the winter solstice. A lot of people think it was a ceremonial location for significant astronomical occurrences.

Take a Guided Tour: An informed guide may enhance your experience by sharing insights into the temple's spiritual importance, architectural design, and history.

5. Temple of The Three Windows

Key Details:
-With three trapezoidal windows offering stunning views of the surroundings, the Temple of the Three Windows is an enchanting building.
- The Incas' sophisticated architectural abilities are shown by the building quality and exact alignment.

Guide:

Architectural Mastery: Take in the flawless masonry, especially around the three windows that encircle the majestic mountains and verdant valleys. It's a fantastic illustration of the Incas' mastery in engineering and design.

Spiritual Significance: Reflect on the possible holy function of this temple in Inca rites and ceremonies. The vistas and setting were probably chosen for their spiritual resonance.

Paradise for Photography: Remember to bring your camera! Some of the most breathtaking vistas in all of Machu Picchu may be seen in the Temple of the Three Windows.

6. The Main Plaza

Key Details:
The Main Plaza, often referred to as the "Hanan" or the "Upper Plaza," functioned as the city's hub and principal meeting spot.
Notable buildings surround it, such as the Principal Temple, the Royal Tomb, and the Temple of the Sun.

Research Guidance:
Historical Center: The Main Plaza is probably where Inca life was most active. Imagine it teeming

with life as pilgrims and residents gathered for rituals and festivities.

Architectural Grandeur: Take in the surrounding buildings' exquisite design and the thoughtful arrangement of each one in the plaza. The Incas' careful planning is evident in the arrangement and design.

Relaxation and Introspection: Spend a minute sitting in the plaza, absorbing the ambience, and considering the importance of this main area of Machu Picchu.

7. The Inca Bridge

Key Details:
The Inca Bridge is a breathtaking example of Inca engineering and their ability to meld buildings and the surrounding environment together. Made of strong bamboo, this unusual rope bridge served as a covert entryway to Machu Picchu in the past.
A short stroll from the main citadel will take you to the fascinating archeological site known as the Inca Bridge.

Research Guidance:
After entering Machu Picchu, you may see the Inca Bridge, which is accessible by a quick and rather

moderate climb from the main citadel. But it's important to know that because of safety concerns and the bridge's brittle state, you cannot cross it.
Although you won't cross the bridge itself, the route that leads to it offers breathtaking views of the surrounding valleys and the Urubamba River, making it a great hike.

8. The Inca Trail

Key Details:
The magnificent Machu Picchu may be reached along the well-known Inca Trail, a hiking adventure of global renown. There are other routes available, but the traditional 4-day journey is the most well-liked. The trip ends in an amazing arrival at Machu Picchu after passing through a variety of environments, including cloud forests, high-altitude mountain passes, and ancient Inca ruins.
The Inca Trail is a highly sought-after journey that provides a deep connection to the area's history and environment.

Research Guidance:
-To hike the Inca Trail, you need a permit. Permits are restricted because of its popularity and the need to control the amount of visitors. The cost of the four-day Inca Trail hike is between $500 and $600. This cost usually covers the services of an

experienced guide, porters for carrying meals and equipment, and camping accommodations.

- Being well-prepared is essential. Because the Inca Trail requires a lot of physical exertion, make sure you buy appropriate hiking equipment, clothes, and consider bringing altitude sickness medications. It is best to travel the path with a trustworthy tour operator who can take care of the logistics and make sure everything goes smoothly and safely.

It is strongly advised that you make reservations for your Inca Trail experience well in advance, particularly if you want to hike during the peak trekking season, which normally lasts from May to September.

9. Agricultural Terraces

Key Details:
- The incredible agricultural prowess of the Inca empire is shown by the Agricultural Terraces at Machu Picchu. These are a collection of painstakingly designed stepping terraces that have practical and decorative uses.

In addition to being useful for farming, the terraces enhance Machu Picchu's general stability and attractiveness.

Research Guidance:

- You are free to go around Machu Picchu's perimeter, exploring the agricultural terraces. As you stroll along them, savor the historical and architectural importance of them.

- The Incas were able to plant crops in the high Andean mountains while minimizing soil erosion because of the clever construction of these terraces. Admire how the design and placement of the terraces made it possible for effective agricultural methods and water distribution.
- As a vital source of food for the residents of Machu Picchu, these terraces were Key to the city's self-sufficiency during the Inca period.

10. The Watchman's Hut

Key Details:
The stone building called Watchman's Hut, or "Guardhouse," is positioned carefully near Machu Picchu's entrance.
It provided guards with a vantage point from which to monitor and manage city entrance, guaranteeing the city's safety and security.

Research Guidance:
- As you approach Machu Picchu, pause to see the Watchman's Hut, which is positioned high above the terraces. Because of its advantageous position,

guards could keep an eye on everyone entering and leaving this hallowed stronghold.

- Offering breathtaking sweeping views of the nearby mountains and valleys, the Watchman's Hut gives visitors a taste of the Andes' natural splendor.

11. Temple of the Condor:

Key Details:
Known as the Temple of the Condor, this striking rock structure is modeled like the spread wings of the condor, an Inca bird of great significance.
Situated in the southern region of Machu Picchu, it is said to have had ceremonial and ritualistic importance for the Inca people.

Research Guidance:
- The unique shape of the temple, which was enhanced by Inca construction and formed by innate rock formations, is evidence of the Incas' capacity to integrate and improve their surroundings.

Consider the site's spiritual importance and its involvement in Inca rites and rituals as you explore this remarkable location. The condor was revered as a symbol of paradise and the afterlife.

- The Temple of the Condor is a superb illustration of how the Incas harmoniously combined their architectural and spiritual beliefs with the natural environment to create a place of prayer and adoration.

12. Intihuatana Stone:

Key Details:
In the heart of Machu Picchu is the Intihuatana Stone, also known as the "Hitching Post of the Sun," a hallowed ceremonial stone.
The name means "Hitching Post of the Sun," and it is said to have functioned as both a location for rites and sacrifices as well as an astronomical observatory.

Research Guidance:
- Look up at the Intihuatana Stone and reflect on its significance to Inca astronomy and religion. The Inca calendar was aligned by using it to monitor astronomical occurrences and observe the sun's location.
The stone's unusual form, which suggests an abstract depiction of the nearby mountains, is evidence of the Incas' close ties to the natural world.
- The Intihuatana Stone is an essential component of any tour to Machu Picchu due to its strategic

placement and historical importance. It provides a glimpse into the complex cosmic knowledge of the Inca culture.

13. Royal Tomb:

Key Details
The Royal Tomb, often referred to as "Tumba Real," is a room within Machu Picchu that is said to have served as an Inca nobleman's hallowed resting place.
The location of this chamber and the items discovered within point to the possibility that it served as a burial site for important people.

Research Guidance:
- Honor the Royal Tomb's spiritual and historical importance by pausing as you enter. This hall is said to have served as a place of honor and memory for Inca aristocracy.

- The location of the chamber and the items and artifacts discovered within provide a unique window into Inca burial practices and beliefs. The Royal Tomb's significance is evidence of Machu Picchu's spiritual and ceremonial significance.

- Keep in mind the historical significance of the location and treat others with respect while you visit.

14. Funerary Rock Hut:

Key Details:
- Situated atop Machu Picchu, the Funerary Rock Hut, also called the "Hut of the Caretaker of the Funerary Rock," is a little stone building.
- This but is connected to the neighboring Funerary Rock, which may have had ceremonial purposes, and might have been the home of a guardian or caregiver.

Research Guidance:
- The Funerary Rock Hut provides a great viewpoint for aerial views of Machu Picchu. The vista is breathtaking and offers a different viewpoint on how the place is laid up.
- The location's connection to the Funerary Rock suggests that the Incas valued it for ceremonial and spiritual purposes. Think about the customs and rituals that may have been here while you investigate the region.
This is a great place for quiet thought and introspection since it's not too busy.

15. Guardhouse Ruins:

Key Details:
The "Ruins of the Guardhouse," or the Guardhouse Ruins, are a group of stone buildings that are located near Machu Picchu's entryway.
These buildings most likely functioned as quarters for the guards in charge of keeping an eye on who may enter the citadel and making sure it was secure.

Research Guidance:
- The Guardhouse Ruins provide a chance to understand the guards' important position and their function in defending this holy city of Machu Picchu.

- These ruins provide a perfect beginning point for your investigation since they are situated near Machu Picchu's entrance. Think about the duties and pursuits of the guards who used to reside here for a while.

- The Guardhouse Ruins provide you with an insight into the defensive and organizational structures of the Inca society.

16. Huayna Picchu Temple

Key Details:
- Situated at the top of Huayna Picchu, the famous mountain rising above Machu Picchu, lies the Huayna Picchu Temple.

The temple's lofty location and expansive views of Machu Picchu and the surrounding area are said to have contributed to its spiritual and ceremonial significance for the Inca people.

Research Guidance:
In addition to your Machu Picchu admission ticket, you'll need to get a special permission in order to access the Huayna Picchu Temple. Reservations must be made in advance since these permits are restricted.

- The trek to the temple is difficult, with small and steep trails. It's Key to prepare physically and have the right hiking equipment.

- After reaching the peak, enjoy the magnificent views one moment at a time. Because of its position, the temple offers a unique viewpoint of Machu Picchu, letting you admire the site's architecture and majesty from above.

17. Temple of the Moon

Key Details:
Situated in the southern region of Machu Picchu, the Temple of the Moon, often referred to as the "Templo de la Luna," is a complex cave-like structure.
It is believed that this mysterious temple was used for rites related to moon worship.

Research Guidance:
- Your standard Machu Picchu admission ticket usually includes access to the Temple of the Moon. It's an interesting place to visit since it provides an alternative viewpoint to the major buildings of the citadel.

- As you explore the temple, pay attention to the detailed rock sculptures and cave nooks. The Incas may have associated these characteristics with ceremonies or spiritual importance.

- The Temple of the Moon offers an insight into the spiritual customs of the Inca society and is a place of silent reflection.

18. Room of the Three Doors:

Key Details:

One of Machu Picchu's most distinctive architectural features is the "Habitación de las Tres Portadas," also known as the Room of the Three Doors.

This chamber, which has three doors, could have been used for administrative or ceremonial purposes.

Research Guidance:
- Your regular admission ticket includes access to the Room of the Three Doors, which is situated in Machu Picchu's urban area.

Due to its three doors and central position in the city, the chamber seems to have been used for major events, meetings, or administrative duties.

- As you stand in this chamber, think about how important it was to the people who lived in Machu Picchu on a daily basis and the possible events that took place here.

19. Sayacmarca Ruins

Key Details:
Sayacmarca, often written Sayacmarka, is an Inca Trail archeological site.

It is said to have functioned as the Incas' ceremonial and administrative hub, with notable architectural elements including agricultural terraces and well-preserved circular structures.

Research Guidance:
- Most itineraries for hikers who follow the Inca Trail to Machu Picchu provide access to Sayacmarca. Both the site's strategic position and the sophisticated Inca masonry are impressive to visitors.

- Consider Sayacmarca's possible uses as a location for administrative and religious events while you tour it. Its name translates to "Inaccessible Town," and the isolation of the place contributes to its importance and mystery.

- The location is a worthwhile halt along the Inca Trail, providing stunning views of the nearby mountains and valleys.

20. Putucusi Mountain

Key Details
The Putucusi Mountain, often called "Happy Mountain," is situated across the Urubamba River from Machu Picchu.
The trek is strenuous and leads to a viewpoint with amazing views of Machu Picchu and the surroundings.

Research Guidance:
- Putucusi Mountain is open to tourists and may be hiked without a specific permission. But the path may be physically taxing due to its steepness.

- The trek is rewarded with breathtaking sweeping vistas of Machu Picchu, offering an unparalleled viewpoint of the fortress from afar.

- Keep in mind the difficult terrain while trekking Putucusi, and make sure you have drink and appropriate boots. The summit's sights are well worth the effort.

21. Inca Drawbridge

Key Details:
On the Inca Trail stands the Inca Drawbridge, also known as "Puente Inca," a historic Inca structure. Although this bridge was formerly a part of the Inca road network, travelers are usually not allowed to cross it because of its brittle nature and potential hazards.

Research Guidance:
- When hiking the Inca Trail, you can often see the Inca Drawbridge from a safe distance. Even though you won't cross it, pause to consider its historical

importance and the technical marvel that is the Inca road network.

- The bridge's construction is evidence of the Inca civilization's capacity to conquer difficult terrain, and its placement was Key for both commerce and defense.

In order to preserve the bridge's delicate condition and guarantee your safety while visiting, keep in mind that access is limited.

22. Wiñay Wayna Ruins

Key Details:
- Wiñay Wayna, often written Winay Wayna, is an archeological site near Machu Picchu that is located along the Inca Trail.

- "Wiñay Wayna" means "Forever Young" or "Eternal Youth" in Quechua, indicating the significance of the location and its function in Inca culture.

Research Guidance:
A usual route for hikers hiking the Inca Trail to Machu Picchu includes access to Wiñay Wayna. The location has religious buildings, ceremonial baths, and terraces that have been maintained.

Examine Wiñay Wayna and reflect on its importance to Inca culture. It could have provided pilgrims traveling to Machu Picchu with a place to sleep as well as a venue for rites and rituals.

- The location is an appropriate endpoint for the Inca Trail before arriving at Machu Picchu, providing stunning views of the surrounding mountains.

23. Machu Picchu Museum

Key Details:
The "Museo de Sitio Manuel Chávez Ballón," another name for the Machu Picchu Museum, is situated in Aguas Calientes, the village at the foot of Machu Picchu.
The museum features relics, displays, and data on the background and importance of Machu Picchu.

Research Guidance:
- Before your visit, visiting the Machu Picchu Museum is a great opportunity to learn more about the location. It sheds light on Machu Picchu's cultural and historical background.

A vast array of objects, including tools, textiles, and pottery, as well as thorough explanations of the history of the site and archeological findings, are on display at the museum.

- A trip to the museum before your trip to Machu Picchu will help you better understand the importance of the location and its role in Inca culture.

24. Machu Picchu Gateway Museum:

The "Museo de Sitio Casa del Guardián," also referred to as the Machu Picchu Gateway Museum, is located close to the site of the entrance.
This little museum offers information about Machu Picchu's past and archeology.

Research Guidance:
- A trip to the Machu Picchu Gateway Museum might serve as an excellent point of departure for exploring the ancient complex. It provides an overview of Machu Picchu's history and importance.

- The museum presents historical details and archeological discoveries, which aid in your comprehension of the cultural and historical background of the location.

It is advisable to visit the museum before visiting Machu Picchu in order to get ready for the immersive experience that takes place within the citadel.

Part B: Fun Things To Do

25. Hike the Inca Trail

Key Details:
- One of the most well-known hiking paths in the world, the Inca Trail leads to Machu Picchu.
- It provides a variety of sceneries, including cloud forests, high-altitude mountain routes, Inca ruins, and the breathtaking arrival at Machu Picchu.

A Special Experience:
Trekking the Inca Trail enables you to walk in the ancient Incas' footsteps as you pass through

breathtaking countryside on stone walkways that have been maintained.

- The trip gives a deep connection to the history and environment of the area and is both a physical and spiritual experience.

26. Explore the Sacred Valley

Key Details:
The Sacred Valley, also known as "Valle Sagrado," is a lush area between Cusco and Machu Picchu that is situated along the Urubamba River.
It offers a variety of activities and is peppered with quaint villages and Inca ruins.

A Special Experience:
- You may explore markets, archeological sites, and communities where the Quechua culture is still vibrant by exploring the Sacred Valley.

- You can take in the breathtaking scenery, try the regional food, and learn about the day-to-day activities of Andean villages.

27. Hike to the Sun Gate:

Key Details:

The Sun Gate, also known as "Inti Punku," is a sacred location on the Inca Trail that provides the first expansive vista of Machu Picchu.
Hikers who like to see the dawn over the citadel often use this trail.

A Special Experience:
You may get a unique perspective of Machu Picchu by hiking to the Sun Gate. The vista at daybreak is breathtaking, with the sun casting a golden glow over the castle.

The trek is very short, and the reward is the famous vista of Machu Picchu from a spot that is generally only accessible by Inca priests.

28. Climb Huayna Picchu

Key Details:
Rising above Machu Picchu is the famous mountain known as Huayna Picchu.
Huayna Picchu climbing is a demanding but very rewarding experience.

A Special Experience:
- Climbing Huayna Picchu offers a distinctive aerial view of Machu Picchu. The citadel will be seen tucked away amid the striking surroundings.

- The climb includes tight, steep trails, historic stone stairs, and an enlightening stop at the Temple of the Moon. Because there is a daily cap on the number of visitors, make sure you get permission in advance.

29. Visit the Putucusi Mountain

Key Details:
- The "Happy Mountain," also known as Putucusi Mountain, is situated across the Urubamba River from Machu Picchu.
- It provides breathtaking panoramic views along with a strenuous trek.

A Special Experience:
- Hiking Putucusi Mountain is an intense yet worthwhile experience. Magnificent views of Machu Picchu and the surroundings may be seen from the peak.
It's a less congested option to Huayna Picchu, and the climb lets you experience the verdant surroundings of a jungle.

30. Trek to the Temple of the Moon:

Key Details:

- The "Templo de la Luna," also known as the Temple of the Moon, is a fascinating cave-like structure close to Machu Picchu.

- You may explore the site's mysterious rooms and carvings by hiking there.

A Special Experience:
- Entering the cave and seeing its elaborate rock carvings and niches gives the hike to the Temple of the Moon an air of adventure.
The temple's setting amid a verdant woodland produces a calm and enchanted ambiance for your investigation.

31. Bird watching in the Cloud Forest:

Key Details:
- A vast array of bird species may be found in the Cloud Forest, which is a component of the Andes' varied environment.
- You may see toucans, hummingbirds, quetzals, and other stunning and unusual bird species while bird watching in this verdant setting.

A Special Experience:
- Discovering the Cloud Forest provides an opportunity to appreciate the richness of the area and establish a connection with nature.

There are options for professional guides to assist you in identifying and seeing these amazing birds, as well as offering insights into their habitats and habits. These trips include bird-watching.

32. River Rafting in Urubamba River:

Key Details:

The "Sacred River," the Urubamba River, provides exhilarating white-water rafting experiences.

The river has parts that are suitable for different skill levels, ranging from serene waters to heart-pounding rapids.

A Special Experience:
- Rafting the Urubamba River is an amazing activity that gives you a different viewpoint on the breathtaking scenery.

- There are alternatives for every skill level of rafter, regardless of experience. It's a thrilling opportunity to take in the breathtaking natural beauty of the area and establish a connection with its strong rivers.

33. Zipline through the Cloud Forest:

Key Details:
Soaring over the trees on a zipline in the Cloud Forest delivers a thrilling sensation.
There are several zip lining courses that provide amazing vistas and varying degrees of severity.

A Special Experience:
- You may obtain an exhilarating perspective of the Cloud Forest by ziplining, which gives you a bird's-eye view of the rich greenery and varied species.

- Experience an exciting connection with nature as you glide over the canopy and take in the surge of wind.

34. Horseback Riding Tours:

Key Details:
Horseback riding excursions provide a more leisurely approach to see the surroundings of Machu Picchu.

There are a number of options available to you, such as trips across the high Andean plains or the Sacred Valley.

A Special Experience:
- Horseback riding trips provide a distinct pace that lets you take your time taking in the area's natural beauty.

- While riding through stunning landscapes, you may explore traditional towns, archeological sites, and other hidden jewels. It's the ideal choice for anyone who likes to have a peaceful connection with nature.

35. Mountain Biking:

Key Details:
- There are several beautiful mountain bike routes in the Machu Picchu area.

- You may experience the excitement of motorcycling while taking in the nearby towns and surroundings.

A Special Experience:
- You can cover more terrain and find hidden jewels that you would miss on foot while mountain riding.

- Enjoy the stunning scenery and a close-up look at Andean culture as you ride through charming valleys, past historic monuments, and beside the Urubamba River.

36. Enjoy a Scenic Picnic:

Key Details:
The Machu Picchu area offers a variety of picturesque locations, including riverbanks and verdant meadows, for picnics.
Bring a picnic or make plans to have one with nearby tour companies, and enjoy a meal in the breathtaking scenery.

A Special Experience:
A peaceful and private way to take in Machu Picchu's scenery is with a picnic.
- While making unique memories in a tranquil location, you may enjoy the local delicacies, take in

the beautiful ambiance, and listen to the sounds of nature.

37. Hot Springs in Aguas Calientes:

Key Details:
- There are naturally occurring hot springs in Aguas Calientes, the settlement at the foot of Machu Picchu.
These hot baths provide the ideal means of relaxation and renewal after your exploration of the historic sites.

A Special Experience:
- Enjoying a therapeutic experience and relaxing your muscles is possible by soaking in the hot springs.
Encircled by rich flora, the hot springs provide a calm location that makes for a relaxing and soothing activity.

38. Attend a Traditional Andean ceremony:

Key Details:
Local shamans provide traditional Andean rites in which you may take part.

Offerings to Pachamama, or Mother Earth, readings from coca leaves, and spiritual blessings are possible components of these rituals.

A Special Experience:
- Attending an Andean ceremony provides a chance to engage with the spiritual practices and beliefs of the Andean people.

You'll learn about their faith, philosophy, and the value of nature in their way of life. It's a significant and distinctive cultural encounter.

39. Visit Local Markets in Aguas Calientes:

Key Details:
There are lively marketplaces in Aguas Calientes, the village at the foot of Machu Picchu.
You may peruse these markets to find handcrafted goods, jewelry, textiles, and other distinctive keepsakes made locally.

A Special Experience:
You may support local craftspeople and interact with the community by going to the markets.
Authentic handmade goods like colorful textiles, traditional ceramics, and products made from

alpaca wool are available, providing it the ideal chance to bring a little of Andean culture home.

40. Learn about Andean Textiles:

Key Details:
Andean textiles are a rich and historic heritage distinguished by their elaborate patterns and vivid hues.
To learn about the craft of Andean textile weaving, take part in workshops or visit villages that weave textiles.

A Special Experience:
Gaining knowledge about Andean textiles helps one appreciate these materials' cultural value on a deeper level.
- You may watch local artists demonstrate their skill as they create beautiful patterns using age-old techniques, or you can try your hand at traditional weaving techniques and create your own one-of-a-kind item.

41. Taste Some Andean Food:

Key Details:

Andean cuisine has a wide range of tastes and often uses local foods like potatoes, quinoa, and alpaca meat.
You may enjoy classic foods like causa, ceviche, and lomo saltado at neighborhood eateries and markets.

A Special Experience:
- Indulging in Andean food is a delectable way to get fully immersed in the culture.
Eating local cuisine is a sensory experience that offers a sense of the Andean culinary legacy and the blending of traditional tastes with contemporary preparation methods.
A wide range of traditional Peruvian meals are available at Machu Picchu and the surrounding areas. The following is a list of several foods you may come across:

1. Ceviche: - Raw fish marinated in lemon or lime juice, often combined with cilantro, onions, and chili peppers.

2. Lomo Saltado: - A stir-fry meal with beef, veggies, and seasonings, frequently eaten with rice.

3. Aji de Gallina: - Creamy, spicy sauce prepared with yellow chili peppers including shredded chicken.

4. Quinoa Soup: – A wholesome soup consisting of quinoa, sometimes meat, and vegetables.

5. Papa a la Huancaína: sliced potatoes in a hot cheese sauce.

6. Alpaca Meat: - A lean and tender substitute is alpaca meat that is grilled or stewed.

7. Anticuchos: - Marinated beef heart is often used to make grilled skewers.

8. Rocoto Relleno: - Hot peppers that are loaded with cheese, meat, or vegetables.

9. Cuy (Guinea Pig): - Typically roasted or fried, this is a classic Andean delicacy.

10. Choclo with Queso: - Cheese served with large-grain corn on the cob.

11. Humitas: - Cheese or meat-filled steamed corn cakes.

12. Pisco Sour: - Made with pisco (grape brandy), lime juice, simple syrup, egg white, and bitters, this is Peru's national drink.

13. Inca Kola: - Well-liked in Peru, this soda is distinguished by its distinct golden hue and delightful flavor.

These are just a few examples of Peru's vast and varied gastronomic landscape. It is probable that you will have the chance to sample a variety of regional specialties and traditional Peruvian cuisine while visiting Machu Picchu and the surrounding locations.

42. Participate in a Pachamama Ceremony:

Key Details:
Andean spirituality is centered on rites honoring Pachamama, the Andean Earth Goddess.
Local shamanic practitioners will lead rituals, music, and offerings throughout these ceremonies, in which you are welcome to take part.

A Special Experience:
- Engaging in a Pachamama ceremony facilitates a spiritual connection with the Andean people.
It's a moving event that highlights the interdependence of all living things and care for the

Earth. The ritual provides a profound understanding of Andean spirituality.

43. Watch Traditional Dance Performances:

Key Details:
Traditional Andean dance performances, which often include vibrant costumes and upbeat music, are an essential aspect of the community's culture.
These shows are available in Aguas Calientes, where they are often accompanied with storytelling and folklore from the area.

A Special Experience:
Enjoying a traditional dance performance is a great way to fully experience the colorful and exuberant elements of Andean culture.
- The engaging dances you'll see will add a dynamic and energetic layer to your cultural experience as they portray the history, agricultural customs, and everyday life of the area.

44. Visit the Museo de Sitio Manuel Chávez Ballón:

Key Details:

The history and archeology of Machu Picchu are the focus of the nearby Museo de Sitio Manuel Chávez Ballón.

Exhibits include images, relics, and comprehensive information regarding the discovery of Machu Picchu and current study.

A Special Experience:
You may get a deeper knowledge of Machu Picchu's history and importance by visiting this museum.
- You may investigate the archeological findings and artifacts that have added to our understanding of this historic fortress, providing you with a comprehensive understanding of its fascinating past.

45. Explore the Orchid Botanical Garden:

Key Details:
A wide range of locally native orchid species may be seen in the Orchid Botanical Garden, which is close to Machu Picchu.

It provides an engaging experience for people who love the outdoors and the distinctive Andean flora.

A Special Experience:

- You may establish a connection with the remarkable biodiversity of the area by exploring the Orchid Botanical Garden.
You'll get to see a variety of orchid species in their native environments and marvel at the delicate beauty of these alluring blooms.

46. Go check out the Butterfly House!

Key Details:
Aguas Calientes' Butterfly House is a conservation institution devoted to regional butterfly species.
It provides informative tours and the opportunity to see and discover the life cycle of these amazing insects.

A Special Experience:
- Especially for children, a visit to the Butterfly House offers an engaging and instructive experience.
- You may see butterflies during different phases of their life cycle, learn about their essential function in the environment, and contribute to conservation efforts.

From taking in traditional dance performances and learning about the history of the site to getting up close and personal with the diverse flora in the Orchid Botanical Garden and discovering the fascinating world of butterflies, these activities offer a wide range of cultural and natural experiences in the Machu Picchu region. Every activity enhances the overall delightful experience of visiting this remarkable location.

47. Sunrise and Sunset Photography:

Key Details:
-Machu Picchu is well known for its magnificent vistas at dawn and dusk, which make for great picture ops.
- Captivating landscapes are created by the way light plays on the ancient ruins and the surrounding mountains.

A Special Experience:
- Witnessing the sun set or dawn in Machu Picchu is a breathtaking sight. The citadel is transformed into a mysterious marvel by the gentle, golden light.
- The site's deep beauty may be captured in spectacular images that you can produce with the shifting hues and shadows.

48. Scenic Views of the Urubamba River:

Key Details:

- The Urubamba River winds through the Sacred Valley, offering stunning views and chances for photography.
- To catch its twisting flow, there are excellent observation spots along its banks or from higher altitudes.

A Special Experience:
Capturing images of the Urubamba River enables you to preserve the breathtaking natural landscape and the vital life-giving waterway that traverses the area.
- The river provides serene and enthralling compositions, surrounded by thick foliage and mountains.

49. Wildlife Photography

Key Details:
- A variety of animals, including birds and mammals like foxes and spectacled bears, may be found in the Machu Picchu area.
- The area's observation spots and guided excursions provide fantastic chances for wildlife photography.

A Special Experience:

- By taking pictures of wildlife, you may interact with the area's rich biodiversity and record unique moments.
- Be ready to capture images of the amazing adaptations of the organisms that survive in this unusual habitat, the vivid feathers of birds, and the secretive movements of mammals.

50. Capture the llamas and Alpacas

Key Details:
Famous Andean emblems, llamas and alpacas, may be seen wandering the Machu Picchu site and its environs.
In addition to being picturesque, they embodie the Andean way of life.

A Special Experience:
- Taking pictures with llamas and alpacas is a cute and entertaining part of your trip.
These kind animals often appear against the background of historic ruin sites, resulting in a very Andean fusion of the past and present.

51. Stunning Agricultural Terraces

Key Details:

- The "andenes," or agricultural terraces, of Machu Picchu are evidence of the Inca civilization's mastery in engineering.

These painstakingly built terraces, grouped in a pleasing symmetry, are a beautiful wonder in addition to being useful.

A Special Experience:
Capturing the elaborate patterns on camera of the agricultural terraces reflects the Incas' strong ties to the earth.

Investigate various viewpoints and angles to highlight the remarkable fusion of artistic creativity and the beauty of the natural world.

52. Ancient Stone Structures:

Key Details:
The well-preserved stone constructions of Machu Picchu, which include plazas, temples, and residential buildings, are well-known.

One of the main characteristics of the site's exceptional architecture is the accuracy and craftsmanship of the Inca masonry.

A Special Experience:
- Preserving the historic rock constructions offers insight into the finer points of Inca artistry.

Pay attention to the distinctive elements, such as the exquisitely carved niches and the skillfully put-together stones that form the amazing stone walls.

53. Misty Mountain Landscapes:

Key Details:
- Mist and fog are common in the Machu Picchu region, giving the area a mysterious feel.
- Your photos take on an intriguing aspect thanks to these dreamy sceneries.

A Special Experience:
- Capturing the foggy alpine scenery with a camera lets you produce surreal and moving pictures.
Accept the moodiness of the weather and utilize the mist to your advantage to give your photos a magical touch.

54. Cloud Forest Flora:

Key Details:
- Machu Picchu's cloud forest is teeming with exotic plants and luxuriant foliage.
- Vibrant wildflowers, ferns, and orchids weave a colorful tapestry.

A Special Experience:
Capturing images of the flora of the cloud forest transports you to the colorful realm of Andean botany.
- Direct your camera's attention to the vibrant hues, delicate shapes, and sophisticated patterns of the many plant species that flourish in this exceptional environment.

55. Train Ride through the Valley:
Key Details:

- The trip to Machu Picchu by train gives beautiful views of the Urubamba Valley.
- The Urubamba River, verdant surroundings, and stunning vistas of the Andes are what make this route so well-known.

A Special Experience:
- Traveling by train is a pleasant and cozy way to take in the breathtaking beauty of the area.
Luxurious carriages allow you to relax while admiring the shifting scenery, which makes it the perfect setting for languid photography.

56. Paragliding over Machu Picchu:

Key Details:
- Seeing Machu Picchu from above by paragliding offers a unique and breathtaking viewpoint of the historic fortress.
There are tandem paragliding flights available for both novice and expert pilots.

A Special Experience:
- Experience an unmatched aerial perspective of Machu Picchu, including the fortress, the encircling peaks, and the verdant valleys, via parachute above the site.

- The exciting encounter is an amazing method to get in touch with the remarkable scenery of this area.

57. Rock Climbing in the Region:

Key Details:
- Adventurers may go rock climbing in the Machu Picchu area.
There are guided rock climbing trips for different ability levels that let you scale the Andes cliffs.

A Special Experience:
- Rock climbing gives your adventure a physically demanding and engaging element that lets you interact with the untamed environments.
- Climb the sheer rock walls, take in the exhilarating experience, and enjoy the satisfying vistas from the top.

58. Explore the Caves Near Machu Picchu:

Key Details:
- There are other fascinating caverns in the area around Machu Picchu, including the Royal caverns and the Temple of the Moon.

Investigating these caverns offers insights on the religious and ceremonial customs of the Inca people.

A Special Experience:
By exploring the caverns, you may go back in time and see the mysterious and sacred locations of the Incas.
You can explore the hidden rooms, find the offerings and sculptures, and learn more about Inca culture.

59. Mountain Biking on Inca Trails:

Key Details:
Mountain riding along Inca Trails is a unique approach to discover historic routes and ruins.
Access to routes like the Inca Jungle Trail, which combine bicycling, trekking, and cultural discovery, is made possible via guided trips.

A Special Experience:
- You may experience the exhilaration of downhill riding while riding mountain bikes on Inca Trails and walking in the Incas' footsteps.
- You'll experience the Andes' natural beauty in a dynamic and thrilling manner as you travel across stunning landscapes and uncover undiscovered archeological sites.

60. Canopy and Zip-lining Adventures:

Key Details:
- Adventures on ziplines and canopy tours take place in the verdant cloud woods close to Machu Picchu.
- You may fly through the trees on a number of ziplines and platforms available for these activities.

A Special Experience:
- Adventures like canopy and zip-lining provide a thrilling way to see the cloud forest's canopy.
Take in the breath-taking scenery and feel the exhilaration of soaring while surrounded by the varied flora and animals of this exceptional environment.

61. White-water rafting in Urubamba River:

Key Details:
- White-water rafting on the Urubamba River is an exciting experience.
There are areas of the river that are appropriate for rafters of all experience levels, with courses that fit both novices and experts.

A Special Experience:

- The Urubamba River provides an exhilarating experience for white-water rafting enthusiasts as they maneuver over rapids and take in the breathtaking scenery.
- As you take in the breathtaking scenery of the Sacred Valley, you'll feel the river's sheer strength.

62. Via Ferrata Climbing and Zipline:

Key Details:
Rock climbing and ziplining are combined into one exciting activity with the Via Ferrata climbing and ziplining tour.
It happens on the Sacred Valley's sheer cliffs.

A Special Experience:
- The Via Ferrata experience provides a unique chance to scale sheer cliff faces while harnessed into a safety net.
- After climbing, you'll have the opportunity to use ziplines to fly over the valley, offering a once-in-a-lifetime experience combining breathtaking scenery with thrilling excitement.

63. Birdwatching in the Cloud Forest:

Key Details:

The cloud forest that envelops Machu Picchu is a haven for avian enthusiasts, harboring a wide variety of birdlife.
There are guided birding trips that provide the chance to see unusual species like tanagers, toucans, and quetzals.

A Special Experience:
- You may establish a connection with the amazing biodiversity of the area by going birdwatching in the Cloud Forest.
- You may take in the vivid plumage of the birds, listen to their beautiful cries, and feel the tranquil ambiance of this verdant setting.

64. Spot Orchids and Native Flora:

Key Details:
The Cloud Forest is well known for its remarkable assortment of native plants, including orchid species.
You may explore and learn about the colorful and delicate world of these exotic plants via guided excursions.

A Special Experience:
Discovering orchids and indigenous plants takes your senses on a sensory adventure through the Cloud Forest's verdant splendor.

- The fine details of ferns, wildflowers, and orchids that combine to form a vibrant and entrancing tapestry may be captured.

65. Llama and Alpaca Encounters:

Key Details:
Famous Andean creatures, llamas and alpacas, are often seen in the Machu Picchu area.
Encounters with these gentle animals reveal more about their significance to the Andean way of life.

A Special Experience:
- Meeting llamas and alpacas provides an opportunity to bond with these endearing and culturally important creatures.
- You may merge tradition and nature by capturing their charming presence against the background of historic ruins.

66. Monkey Watching in the Forest:

Key Details:
A variety of monkey species, including spectacled bears and brown capuchins, call the Cloud Forest home.
Observatories and guided excursions provide chances to see these gregarious and inquisitive animals.

A Special Experience:
- Witnessing monkeys in their natural environment is an exciting experience.
- You may get a closer understanding of the ecology by seeing their social relationships, acrobatic displays, and interactions with the forest.

From the melodic world of birding in the Cloud Forest and finding the bright orchids and local flora to engaging with llamas, alpacas, and the charming presence of monkeys, these activities provide a rich tapestry of interactions and observations in the Machu Picchu area. Every encounter deepens and broadens your understanding of this remarkable place.

67. Butterfly Spotting:

Key Details:
A sanctuary for butterfly fans, the Machu Picchu area is home to a vast range of butterfly species.
You may get up close and personal with these elegant insects by taking guided excursions or visiting butterfly sanctuaries.

A Special Experience:

- Seeing butterflies gives you a chance to fully immerse yourself in their vibrant and delicate world.
- As they fly around the verdant surroundings, you can see their colorful patterns, soft flight, and demeanor.

68. Andean Condor Watching:

Key Details:
The towering mountain ranges in the area are home to the Andean condor, one of the biggest flying birds in the world.
Opportunities to see these magnificent animals in their native environment are offered by guided tours and observation points.

A Special Experience:
- Observing Andean condors gives you an intimate glimpse into the formidable and breathtaking world of these recognizable birds.
- Watch them soar over the Andes peaks on thermals, showcasing their enormous wingspan and exquisite flight.

69. Soak in the Aguas Calientes Hot Springs:

Key Details:
The settlement at the foot of Machu Picchu, Aguas Calientes, is well-known for its natural hot springs.
After a day of seeing the ancient sites, unwind and revitalize yourself by soaking in the hot springs.

A Special Experience:
A tranquil approach to relax is to soak in the hot springs, which are surrounded by verdant foliage and the calming sounds of the natural world.
In addition to providing therapeutic advantages, the experience infuses your journey with a hint of calm.

70. Yoga and Meditation Retreats:

Key Details:
Mindfulness and self-discovery-focused yoga and meditation retreats are available in the Machu Picchu area.
Calm surroundings and knowledgeable teachers provide the perfect backdrop for introspection.

A Special Experience:

- Immerse yourself in the tranquil beauty of the Andes by signing up for a yoga and meditation retreat.
In the peaceful surroundings, you can engage in mindfulness practices, embrace relaxation techniques, and discover a sense of balance and renewal.

71. Spa and Wellness Centers:

Key Details:
There are several spas and wellness facilities in the Machu Picchu region that promote rest and renewal.
Services to help you relax and reenergize include hot stone treatments, massages, and yoga classes.

A Special Experience:
- Spas and wellness facilities provide a haven where you can relax and treat yourself.
- To revitalize your body and mind, indulge in holistic wellness practices or massages influenced by ancient Inca traditions.

72. Forest Bathing in the Cloud Forest:

Key Details:

"Shinrin-yoku," also known as "forest bathing," is the practice of spending time in nature to lower stress and improve wellbeing.

The Cloud Forest's verdant, peaceful surroundings make it the perfect place to conduct this exercise.

A Special Experience:
- By taking a forest bathe in the Cloud Forest, you can feel the therapeutic effects of the forest and establish a close connection with nature.
- You may engage your senses, listen to the sounds of the forest, smell the fresh air, and find calm amid the greenery.

73. Aguas Calientes Town Exploration:

Key Details:
Aguas Calientes is the town at the foot of Machu Picchu and has its own particular charm.

Exploring the town enables you to explore local stores, restaurants, and the lively center market.

A Special Experience:
- Aguas Calientes town is a lively center that mixes contemporary conveniences with a unique Andean flavor.
- You can experience local food, browse for souvenirs, and enjoy the bustling environment before or after your Machu Picchu journey.

74. Explore Ollantaytambo:

Key Details:
Ollantaytambo is a historic town in the Sacred Valley, famed for its well-preserved Inca architecture.
Exploring Ollantaytambo gives insights on Inca urban design and the town's significance as a military, religious, and agricultural hub.

A Special Experience:
- Exploring Ollantaytambo offers you a stroll through time, with its old alleyways and spectacular stone constructions.
- You may explore ancient sites like the Ollantaytambo Fortress and discover the rich history and culture of the area.

75. Visit Pisac and its Market:

Key Details:
Known for its vibrant market, Pisac is a charming village in the Sacred Valley.
The market is an ideal destination for souvenir shopping since it has a vast selection of handicrafts, textiles, jewelry, and local products.

A Special Experience:
- Immersion in Andean culture may be had by visiting Pisac and its market.
Engage with regional artists, peruse colorful booths, and discover one-of-a-kind handmade goods that honor the area's rich customs.

76. Discover Chinchero Village:

Key Details:
Chinchero is a classic Andean community renowned for its colonial architecture and restored Inca terraces.
The community serves as a starting point for learning about Andean customs, such as agriculture and weaving.

A Special Experience:
- Learning about Chinchero village provides insights into the way of life and cultural legacy of Andeans.
- You may tour the quaint streets that haven't lost their ancient beauty, see textile demonstrations, and go to the neighborhood church.

77. Explore Urubamba Village:

Key Details:

- The Sacred Valley's Urubamba is a little village renowned for its tranquil environment.
- It is the location of charming cafés and restaurants and acts as a starting point for visiting the nearby ancient sites.

A Special Experience:
- Discovering Urubamba village lets you experience Andean living at a slower pace.
Enjoy the regional food, unwind in the main plaza, and use it as the jumping off point for a variety of local adventures.

78. Santa Teresa Village:

Key Details:
Situated in the verdant valley of the Vilcabamba mountain range lies the charming town of Santa Teresa.
It has hot springs for relaxing and serves as the beginning of the alternate Inca Trail.

A Special Experience:
The town of Santa Teresa is a haven of peace and stunning scenery.
- Take part in strenuous hikes, relax in the revitalizing hot springs, and discover the secluded allure of the Andean mountains.

79. Hike to Santa Teresa Hot Springs:

Key Details:
Tucked away in the Andes highlands are the naturally occurring thermal springs of Santa Teresa.
The trip to the hot springs is beautiful and offers a gratifying chance to unwind amid verdant scenery.

A Special Experience:
- Trekking through the peaceful forest to reach Santa Teresa Hot Springs is a lovely experience.
Surrounded by the unspoiled splendor of the Andes, you may relax in the healing hot springs.

80 . Explore the Maras Salt Ponds:

Key Details:
Dating back to pre-Inca times, the Maras salt ponds are a network of hundreds of salt pools.
A historically significant and aesthetically pleasing location, the elaborate terraces are still employed for the extraction of salt.

A Special Experience:
You can see how salt is made, a process that has been going on for millennia, by exploring the Maras salt ponds.

- You may wander around the colorful tiered ponds and see how the salt crystallization forms distinctive patterns.

81. Visit Moray Agricultural Terraces:

Key Details:
An archaeological site called the Moray Agricultural Terraces is home to a sequence of concentric terraces that were constructed into a naturally occurring depression.
- The terraces are an amazing example of Inca engineering and were probably utilized for agricultural research.

A Special Experience:
- Exploring the Moray agricultural terraces provides insight into the agricultural inventiveness and methods used by the Incas.
- You can examine the peculiar circular design and recognize the microclimates that the Incas used to support a variety of crops.

82. Explore the Ruins of Ollantaytambo

Key Details:

There are several Inca remains at Ollantaytambo, including temples, agricultural terraces, and a fort.
The location's significance in Inca history and its well-preserved Inca architecture make it noteworthy.

A Special Experience:
- Exploring this active Inca village and learning about the Ollantaytambo Ruins is like taking a trip back in time.
- You can explore the sun temple, scale the spectacular terraces, and understand the site's strategic importance in Inca history.

83. Nighttime Stargazing Tours

Key Details:
The Machu Picchu area provides excellent astronomy conditions with a clean, clear sky.
Stargazing excursions with guides give you the chance to see planets, constellations, and other celestial delights.

A Special Experience:
Take a stargazing tour at night to experience a site of natural and historical value while connecting with the universe.

- While studying the astronomy and cosmology of the ancient Andes, you may look at the stars, planets, and Milky Way.

84. Learn About Inca Astronomy

Key Details:
The Incas possessed a thorough grasp of astronomy, and they intimately linked celestial occurrences to their ceremonies and buildings.
Expert lectures and guided workshops can teach you about Inca astronomy.

A Special Experience:
Understanding Inca astronomy offers insights into the sky knowledge of the prehistoric society.
- You may learn about Machu Picchu's and other Inca monuments' astronomical importance and respect their relationship to the universe.

85. Take a Guided Tour of Machu Picchu

Key Details:
Machu Picchu is a large archeological monument with amazing architecture, a complicated layout, and historical importance.

A guided tour improves your comprehension of the layout, history, and purpose of the place.

A Special Experience:
- A guided tour of Machu Picchu provides an organized and educational look around the fortress.
- You may learn more about the site's elaborate design, hear the historical histories, and find hidden jewels.

86. Hire a Local Guide for In-depth Insights:

Key Details:
- Local guides in the Machu Picchu region have extensive understanding of the region's natural history, culture, and environment.
- Hiring a local guide guarantees an interesting and individualized tour of the area's sights.

A Special Experience:
- Engaging a local guide offers the chance to learn more about the Andes' history and culture.
- You may interact with the locals and learn about their experiences, as well as get in-depth knowledge and uncover lesser-known locations.

These adventures provide a unique combination of awe-inspiring views of the stars, cultural enrichment, and historical insight in the Machu Picchu area. Every activity strengthens your bond with this remarkable place, from learning about Inca astronomy and stargazing at night to taking guided tours of Machu Picchu and hiring local guides for in-depth insights.

87. Attend Workshops and Lectures:

Key Details:
Lectures and seminars on a range of subjects, from environmental conservation to history and archeology, are often held in the Machu Picchu area.

These seminars, which are usually conducted by specialists, provide insightful information on the history and culture of the area.

A Special Experience:
- You may learn more about the Machu Picchu area by attending lectures and workshops.
- You may converse with informed speakers, pose inquiries, and take part in debates that expand your horizons.

88. Visit the Local Schools and Communities:

Key Details:
Visiting nearby settlements and schools offers a glimpse into the everyday existence of the Andean people.
It's a chance to get familiar with their traditions, customs, and struggles.

A Special Experience:
Making relationships and promoting cultural exchange by visiting nearby schools and communities.
You may engage with locals, see community initiatives, and recognize the value of sustainable tourism in bolstering these regions.

89. Attend Workshops on Traditional Andean Pottery:

Key Details:
Practical ceramics creation is provided by traditional Andean pottery studios.
Participants are guided by skilled artists through the shaping, painting, and fire of pottery.

A Special Experience:
Participating in ceramics classes gives you access to the Andes' rich creative legacy.
- You may make your own pottery, learn about the skill involved, and take home a one-of-a-kind memento.

90. Learn about Andean Agriculture:

Key Details:
- The history and culture of the Andes are fundamentally shaped by agriculture.
- You may take part in instructional courses that go over crop production, conventional agricultural methods, and the significance of sustainable agriculture.

A Special Experience:
Understanding Andean agriculture may help one better understand the complex interrelationship that exists between the people and the land.
- You may see the viability of these traditional agricultural techniques by participating in practical activities like planting and harvesting crops.

91. Traditional Andean Cooking Classes:

Key Details:
- Hands-on learning about Andean food is provided via traditional cooking lessons.
- Expert chefs lead participants in the production of regional meals made using products found in the area.

A Special Experience:
- You may explore the cuisines of the Andes by taking cookery lessons.
- You may cook regional specialties like alpaca stew, quinoa soup, and ceviche to forge a stronger connection with the area's culinary history.

92. Spanish Language Classes:

Key Details:
- Visitors who want to become better at the language may take Spanish language courses in the Machu Picchu area.
- Customized instruction, cultural immersion, and the opportunity to interact with locals are all provided by these sessions.

A Special Experience:

Enrolling in Spanish language courses facilitates deeper conversations within the community.
- You may build genuine relationships with the individuals you meet, improve your communication abilities, and comprehend regional cultures.

93. Check for Local Festivals and Events:

Key Details:
- The Machu Picchu area has a number of festivals and events all year long.
You may schedule your visit to take place during events, such as religious festivals or cultural get-togethers, by looking up the local event calendars.

A Special Experience:
- Experiencing the colorful customs of the Andes may be gained by going to local festivals and events.
- You may take part in the happy mood that permeates these events, see colorful processions, music, and dancing.

94. Inti Raymi (Festival of the Sun):

Key Details:

One of the biggest Inca festivals is Inti Raymi, or the Festival of the Sun.

The celebration, which offers a replica of Inca ceremonies, celebrates the winter solstice on June 24.

A Special Experience:
- Experiencing the ancient Inca customs of Inti Raymi is a once-in-a-lifetime opportunity.
- You may take part in a cultural event that highlights the rich legacy of the Andes, watch intricate rituals, and see vibrant costumes.

95. Cusco's Annual Celebrations:

Key Details:
Cusco, the former Inca Empire capital, has a number of yearly festivities and celebrations.

These festivities include colorful processions, music, and dancing, and include Inti Raymi, the Feast of Corpus Christi, and the Cusco Anniversary Festival.

A Special Experience:
- Immersing yourself in Cusco's rich cultural legacy is possible by attending the city's yearly events.
- You may take part in the lively ambiance that defines these celebrations, see vibrant parades, and see people dressed traditionally.

96. Buy Traditional Andean Textiles:

Key Details:
- The Machu Picchu area is well known for its handwoven indigenous textiles, which are created by talented craftsmen.
- As mementos of your travels, you may buy textiles like blankets, scarves made of alpaca, and fabrics with beautiful designs.

A Special Experience:
- Purchasing traditional Andean textiles enables you to support regional craftspeople and carry genuine Andean culture home.
You can see how these fabrics, each with a distinct pattern and significance, are expertly crafted and colorful.

97. Purchase Handmade Crafts:

Key Details:
- Handmade goods such as jewelry, woodworking, and ceramics may be found at a variety of local markets and stores.
- By buying these crafts, you can contribute to the regional economy and bring home one-of-a-kind, handmade mementos.

A Special Experience:
- Purchasing handcrafted goods allows you to interact with the Andean people's ingenuity and workmanship.
- You may stroll around the marketplaces, bargain for one-of-a-kind items, and take home a memento of your trip in the area.

98. Unique Machu Picchu Souvenirs:

Key Details:
A range of distinctive mementos that encapsulate the spirit of the archeological site are available from Machu Picchu.
Miniature reproductions of Machu Picchu, artwork with Andean themes, and other keepsakes commemorating your stay are examples of souvenirs.

A Special Experience:
- Investing in distinctive mementos from Machu Picchu helps you to recall your trip to this famous location.
- As enduring mementos of your trip, you may purchase goods that capture the majesty and magic of Machu Picchu.

99. Plan Your Next Adventure in the Andes:

Key Details:
The Andes mountain range provides an abundance of breathtaking scenery, historical monuments, and cultural experiences.
Organizing your next trip to the Andes might include hiking to inaccessible sites, discovering undiscovered treasures, and taking in the rich cultural diversity of the region.

A Special Experience:
It is an exciting possibility to plan your next excursion in the Andes since it will enable you to learn more about the history and natural beauty of the area. You may plan routes, investigate new places, and look forward to the amazing adventures this magnificent mountain range has in store.

100. Explore Other Inca ruins in Peru:

Key Information:
In addition to Machu Picchu, Peru is home to a multitude of other Inca monuments, each with a distinct history and allure. You may find lesser-known gems like Ollantaytambo,

Sacsayhuaman, and Pisac by exploring other Inca sites.

Unique Experience:
- A greater comprehension of the extensive Inca culture may be gained by visiting further Inca sites in Peru. Marvel at the architectural achievements, discover their historical importance, and take in the nation's rich array of Inca legacy.

101. Visit Cusco, the Historic Capital of the Inca Empire:

Key Details:
- Cusco, dubbed the "Belly Button of the World," served as the Inca Empire's center. You can enjoy Cusco's dynamic cultural scene, architecture, and rich history by going there.

Unique Experience:
- Immersion in the Inca Empire's and Spanish colonial influence's live history is possible while visiting Cusco. You may see the Inca walls, stroll through the historic alleyways, go to the Qoricancha temple, and take in the blend of Spanish and Andean cultures.

Extend your exploration of this amazing area by organizing your next excursion in the Andes, seeing additional Inca monuments in Peru, and traveling to Cusco, the ancient capital of the Inca Empire. Every task presents a fresh chapter in your study of the Andes and Peru's rich cultural heritage.

102. Explore the Amazon Rainforest:

Key Information:
-Only a short flight from Cusco, the Amazon Rainforest provides an unspoiled natural setting with unrivaled biodiversity. There are possibilities to see animals, go on river cruises, climb through jungles, and interact with local tribes while exploring the Amazon.

Unique Experience: Discovering the Amazon Rainforest is like diving into one of the most essential and diversified ecosystems on the planet. You may see beautiful vegetation, get up close and personal with animals like macaws, monkeys, and jaguars, and discover indigenous cultures and their sustainable way of life.

Trekking to Salkantay or Ausangate is a demanding and rewarding trip.

103. Trek to Salkantay or Ausangate:

Beautiful mountain vistas, glistening lakes, and a genuine Andean experience can be found on both treks.

Unique Experience:
Hiking through the high-altitude wilderness to reach Salkantay or Ausangate is an exciting adventure. You will be rewarded with expansive vistas and unspoiled natural beauty after conquering mountain passes and camping under starry sky.

104. Visit Lake Titicaca:

Key Details:
Lake Titicaca is the highest navigable lake in the world and a significant cultural site. You may tour Lake Titicaca's islands, interact with indigenous populations, and discover their way of life by going there.

Unique Experience:
Exploring Lake Titicaca exposes visitors to Andean customs as well as the tranquil beauty of the lake. You may take in the area's rich cultural legacy, see floating reed islands, and communicate with the Uros people.

105. Go sandboarding in Huacachina:

Key Details:
Huacachina is a desert oasis encircled by enormous sand dunes. The thrilling feeling of riding a board down the dunes is provided by sandboarding.

Sandboarding in Huacachina is an exhilarating experience in the middle of the desert. Unique Experience: Glide over the dunes, experience an exhilarating thrill, and take in this natural oasis' distinctive scenery.

These encounters provide access to Peru's varied landscapes and exciting new experiences. Every experience you have when visiting the culturally diverse Lake Titicaca, venturing into the Amazon Rainforest, completing high-altitude climbs, or sandboarding in Huacachina enhances your understanding of this fascinating nation.

Conclusion:

So, dear traveler, I hope this straight-to-the-point guide has stoked your spirit of wonder and adventure as you go out to discover the magnificent splendor of Machu Picchu and beyond. The Machu Picchu area is a place of great importance and limitless exploration because of its historic fortress, stunning scenery, and cultural riches.

I hope your travels bring you to the center of the Andes, where you may marvel at the amazing Machu Picchu Citadel and all around it. I hope you get fully engrossed in the rich history and culture of the Andes, creating links between the past and the present.

Don't let your adventure stop there, however. From the depths of the Amazon Rainforest to the dizzying heights of Salkantay and Ausangate, from the tranquil beaches of Lake Titicaca to the exhilarating sands of Huacachina, the Andes offer a wide range of experiences. Every location has distinct tales and experiences that are just waiting for you to discover.

May you embrace the customs, tastes, and inventiveness of the Andean people as you travel across this amazing country. I hope you enjoy the yearly celebrations and the vibrant culture that envelops the Andes in song and color.

May all of your trips be safe and filled with wonderful moments of self-discovery and joy.

With best regards,

Amy T. Moore.

MACHU PICCHU
CHECKLIST

SHELTER:

COOKING:

CLOTHING

PERSONAL ITEMS:

MACHU PICCHU

MISCELLANEOUS

MACHU PICCHU

My trip BUDGET PLANNER

MONTH

JAN　FEB　MAR　APR　MAY　JUN　JUL　AUG　SEP　OCT　NOV　DEC

TOTAL TRIP BUDGET

DATE	DESCRIPTION	AMOUNT
	TOTAL:	

ESTIMATED TRIP EXPENSES

DATE	DESCRIPTION	AMOUNT
	TOTAL:	

TOTALING

TOTAL INCOME	TOTAL EXPENSES	TOTAL SAVING

BUDGET NOTES　　　*Machu Picchu!*

Printed in Great Britain
by Amazon